servicenow
Best Practices

Authors' Profile

Muhammad Zeeshan Ali

PMP, PMI-ACP, SA, CSA, OCP

Zeeshan is a prolific author with a wealth of experience spanning over 22 years in managing a diverse array of mid to large-scale projects across both Public and Private sectors. His expertise extends to various domains including Agile framework, Traditional Project Management, Performance Management, PMO, Leadership, Team Building, and Personal Motivation. He is renowned for pioneering the innovative "Performance Measurement Matrix," a groundbreaking tool for quantifying performance metrics for both individual software engineers and teams.

A staunch advocate for Agile methodologies, processes, and team skill enhancement, Zeeshan has demonstrated proficiency in managing multiple complex projects concurrently, often with teams dispersed across different geographical locations. He holds a Master's degree in Project Management, a Bachelor's degree in Computer Sciences, and is recognized as a Project Management Professional (PMP) and Agile Certified Professional (PMI-ACP) by the Project Management Institute (PMI), USA. Additionally, he is a Certified SAFe 6 Agilist (SA) by Scaled Agile and a Certified System Administrator (CSA) by ServiceNow.

Saqib Javed John

PMP, PMI-ACP, CSA, ITIL, SCJP, SCWCD, FIDIC

Saqib is one of the founding members and Managing Director of Organizational Governance Management Consultants (OGMC). He has professional expertise of more than 18 years of working on enterprise projects in various business domains ranging from a functional organization to project-based organization.

Saqib has immense experience in developing and managing human behavior, process engineering and optimization, risk management, conflict management, performance maturity audits and policy-making. This is one of the reasons he is relatable to readers of Business and management professions. He is best known for his rapid-learning techniques and easy methods of practical implementations. He also has contributed to many anthologies. His work is helping thousands of students, teachers and professionals.

Saqib is MS (IT), certified "Project Management Professional" (PMP) and "Agile Certified Practitioner" (ACP) from Project Management Institute (PMI) USA. He is also certified in "Information Technology Infrastructure Library" (ITIL) from Exin UK, "Sun Certified Java Programmer" (SCJP) and "Sun Certified Web Component Developer" (SCWCD) from Sun Microsystems USA.

servicenow
Best Practices

Muhammad Zeeshan Ali
PMP, PMI-ACP, SA, CSA, OCP

Saqib Javed John
PMP, PMI-ACP, CSA, ITIL, SCJP, SCWCD

2024

All inquiries should be addressed to (e-mail): publications@tecman.academy

First Printing: 2024

ISBN: 9798324789824

Ordering Information:
Special discounts are available on quantity purchases by corporations, associations, educators, and others. For details, contact the publisher at the above-listed address.

Dedicated to all the readers

and

those who inspired this work.

Preface

In today's dynamic digital landscape, where organizations strive to optimize efficiency, streamline processes, and deliver exceptional services, ServiceNow stands out as a transformative platform driving innovation and excellence. As businesses increasingly rely on ServiceNow to manage their IT, HR, customer service, and other critical functions, the need for best practices has never been more pressing.

This book is a culmination of insights, experiences, and expert advice gathered from seasoned ServiceNow professionals and practitioners. It serves as a comprehensive guide to navigating the complexities of the ServiceNow ecosystem, offering practical strategies and proven methodologies to help organizations harness the full potential of the platform.

Whether you are a ServiceNow administrator, developer, architect, or business leader, this book is your trusted companion on the journey to success. Each chapter is carefully crafted to cover a specific aspect of ServiceNow implementation, from planning and design to configuration, customization, and beyond.

Through real-world examples, case studies, and hands-on exercises, we explore best practices for leveraging ServiceNow to drive digital transformation, enhance service delivery, and achieve business objectives. From optimizing workflows and automating processes to ensuring scalability and security, this book equips you with the knowledge and tools needed to thrive in today's competitive landscape.

As ServiceNow continues to evolve and expand its capabilities, staying abreast of best practices is essential for staying ahead of the curve. Whether you are just beginning your ServiceNow journey or looking to refine your existing practices, this book provides invaluable insights and guidance to help you unlock the full potential of the platform.

We invite you to embark on this journey with us as we explore the best practices that are shaping the future of ServiceNow and empowering organizations to achieve new heights of success.

About TecMan

TecMan Academy operates under the umbrella of OGMC (Organizational Governance Management Consultants). As specialists in ServiceNow, we offer a comprehensive range of expertise including Technical Consulting, Product Training, Implementation, and Application Administration. Our aim is to empower your organization with cutting-edge solutions, modernizing operations and fostering innovation throughout your entire IT infrastructure via a contemporary cloud-based platform.

Executing a successful transformation requires meticulous planning, administration, and setup. We deliver a holistic approach, supplying the necessary expertise, processes, and tools to streamline and automate your digital workflows and business operations.

Understanding the paramount importance of efficiency, our consultants leverage predictive intelligence to ensure timely and cost-effective implementation of solutions tailored to your specific requirements.

Visit our websites for more information:

ogmcs.com

tecman.academy

Table of Contents

1. Why ServiceNow?

- Customization and Flexibility

- Seamless Integrations

- Cognitive AI Capabilities

- Robust Security

- Community Support

- Continual Service Improvement

2. ServiceNow Benefits

- Streamlined Scalability & Workflows

- Improved Service Delivery

- Risk Mitigation

- Lower Operational Costs

- Real-Time Analytics & Dashboards

3. ServiceNow Platform

- Application Platform as a Service (aPaaS)

- Enterprise Level Utilization

- AI & Automation

- Out of the Box (ITIL) Processes

- Well Integrated

- Successful Governance Model

4. ServiceNow Architecture

- Cloud Based Computing Model

- Multi Instance Layers

- Single Data Design

- Highly Available Data Centers

- Frequent Backups

5. ServiceNow Best practices – General planning

- Become familiar with ServiceNow features.

- Leverage all sources of information about the ServiceNow platform.

- Leverage rapid prototyping.

- Use different color schemes for each instance.

- Document your procedure for migrating data.

- Know when to create or modify objects on the system.

6. Essential Best Practices for ServiceNow Smooth Operations

- Build a clear and detailed roadmap

- Don't leave any team behind

- Prefer configurations over customizations

- Train your staff

- Get the experts involved

7. ITSM Main Modules

- Incident Management

- Problem Management

- Change Management

- Service Request Management

- Enterprise Service Management

- Release Management

- Service Level Management

8. Ways to Interact

- Native UI (Next Experience Unified Navigation)

- Mobile Interface

- Portal Interface

- Agent Workspace

- Now Learning Platform

- ServiceNow Community

- ServiceNow Global Events

- ServiceNow Developer Site

9. ITSM Life Cycle

- Strategy

- Design

- Transition

- Operation

- Cont. Improvement

10. ITSM Resolves following Challenges

- Misalignment

- Outdated Legacy

- Manual Processes

- Inefficient Workflows

- Rapid Changes

- Technology Implementation

- Siloes Applications

11. ITOM Main Modules

- Discovery

- Service Mapping

- CMDB

- Event Management

- Health Log Analytics

- Cloud Accelerate

- Metric Intelligence (Operations Management Intelligence)

12. ITOM Life Cycle

- Planning and Definition

- Implementation and Configuration

- Operation and Optimization

- Review and Refinement

- Automate-> Optimize -> Manage

13. ITOM Resolves following Challenges

- Data Management & Efficiency

- DevOps & Collaboration

- Scaling Ops & Pace

- Performance & Productivity

- Availability & Visibility

- Uptime & Utilization

- Downtime & Noise

14. HRSD Main Modules

- HR Case and Knowledge Management

- Employee Service Center

- Lifecycle Events

- HR Integrations

- HR Performance Analytics

- Employee Document Management

- Mobile Onboarding app

15. HRSD Life Cycle

- Planning and Analysis

- Design and Configuration

- Deployment and Training

- Ongoing Management and Improvement

16. HRSD Resolves following Challenges

- Bridging

- Identify Resources needs

- Retaining IT Talent

- Resource Optimization

- Cost Control

- User Experience & Agility

- Employee Innovation Rate

17. ITAM Main Modules

- Software Asset Management

- Hardware Asset Management

- Cloud Insights

- Enterprise Asset Management

- SaaS License Management

- Asset Management Executive Dashboard

- Asset Onboarding and Off boarding

18. ITAM Life Cycle

- Planning

- Acquisition Request

- Fulfill

- Deployment

- Monitor

- Service Management

- Retire / Disposing

19. ITAM Resolves following Challenges

- Data Accuracy & Data Loss

- Diverse and Distributed Assets

- Hybrid Environments

- Visibility of Inventory

- Vulnerability & cyberattacks

- Asset Discovery Rate

- Resource Allocation

20. CSM Main Modules

- Predictive Intelligence

- Guided Decisions

- Virtual Agent

- Agent Workspace

- Advanced Work Assignment

- Omni-channel

21. CSM Life Cycle

- Plan

- Design

- Implement

- Operate

- Optimize

22. CSM Resolves following Challenges

- User Satisfaction

- Navigating

- Data Privacy

- Data Accuracy

- Data Breach

- Self-Service Capabilities

- Multi-Channel Communication

23. GRC Main Modules

- Policy & Compliance

- Risk Management

- Audit Management

- Vendor Risk Management

- Privacy Management

- Regulatory Change Management

- Continuous Authorization & Monitoring

24. GRC Life Cycle

- Draft

- Review

- Awaiting approval

- Published

- Retired

25. GRC Resolves following Challenges

- Strategic Alignment

- Business Goal

- Compliance

- Total Cost of Ownership

- Digital Transformation

- Risk Response Strategies

- Budget & ROI

26. Strategic Portfolio Management (SPM)

- Faster time to market

- Improved response time to disruptions

- Better alignment between strategy and execution

- Improved efficiency

- Cohesion of multiple disciplines

- Increased agility

- Improved speed overall

27. ServiceNow Requirement Gathering Techniques & Best Practices

- Observations & Brainstorming

- Document Analysis, Interface Analysis & Prototyping

- Determine the Right Participants

- Requirements Workshop

- Stakeholders Engagement

- Prioritize the requirements

- Get confirmation of the requirements

28. ServiceNow Analysis Techniques & Best Practices

- Descriptive, Diagnostic, Predictive & Prescriptive Analytics

- SWOT (Strength, Weakness, Opportunity, and Threat)

- MOST (Mission, Objectives, Strategies, and Tactics) Analysis

- PESTLE Analysis (Political, Economic, Sociological, Technological, Legal, Environmental)

- CATWOE (Customers, Actors, Transformation, World View, Owner, Environmental)

- MoSCoW ((Must or Should, Could or Would)

- Brainstorming, Six Thinking Hats, Mind Mapping

29. Configuration Management Best Practices

- Identify your CIs

- Populate your CMDB

- Manage your CI Lifecycle

- Optimize your CI Relationships

- Align your CIs with your Services

- Configuration Change Tracking

- Configuration Versioning and Labelling

30. ServiceNow Development Best Practices

- Proper Naming Conventions for Variables, Tables, Fields etc.

- Code Sensitivity, Document and Comment Code to raise its Credibility

- Always capture your updates in the right Update Set and application scope

- Don't delete any record, Scripts, Business Rules etc. without multiple confirmations in writing

- Instance Sensitivity: Always review your code before deploying it to production environment.

- While writing the scripts make the code organized and well formatted

- Use Modular or Functional programming in order to make the code DRY (Don't Repeat Yourself)

31. ServiceNow Testing Best Practices

- Test system holistically including integration, business-critical flow and configuration changes

- Create Test Plans and the time frame in which the test plan must be run test cases

- Decompose Test Plans further into Test Sets, Test Steps and Test Cycles

- Execute Tests, Evaluate Tests, Assess Test results, test results traceability/tracking

- Run a single test at a time, report defects and retest, if needed

- Create multiple versions of a test describing how a product or feature is to be tested completely

- Ability to document test cases, record test results and troubleshoot errors

32. Benefits of Automated Testing

- Replaces Manual Testing

- Reusable Test Cases

- Reduces human errors

- Quality of client deliverables

- Accelerate Testing Process

33. ServiceNow Deployment Best Practices

- Define Deployment Roadmap, Process, and Activities (including Post-Deployment Support)

- Make compatibility check, prefer Built-in configurations and understand the Impact

- Address Stakeholder Concerns

- Define clearly short and long-term goals

- Go Live gradually, start small and then scale up

- Focus on Deployment Quality

- Post Deployment, Train End-users

34. ServiceNow Customization Best Practices

- No Code and low-code capabilities, Use smart workbooks, Create tests for all customizations

- Prefer UI policies over client scripts, Flow Designer over business rule scripts, IntegrationHub over custom integrations

- Customization should be business-smart, Use scoped applications as your default for any new custom development

- Define demand and avoid using the same names as out-of-the-box objects, methods, or classes.

- Document all customizations, explain why you customized (including business justification), define customization

- Use Health Scan regularly to identify unnecessary customizations, Audit Customization

- Revert to out-of-the-box and Merge your customization with the base system to resolve conflict

35. ServiceNow Integration Best Practices

- Avoid manual intervention and disruption, as manual data entry is a huge drain as its time consuming and error-prone

- Minimize Technical Debt and Automated Workflow Integration, Load Test Each Integration Thoroughly and Separately

- Define integration needs and design, avoid over-engineering and over-customizing the platform

- Collaborate with key stakeholders, Capture integration's requirements, Determine business-driven integration goals

- Map how the integration will work, Consider the impact of the integration on the end-user

- Good Preparation and Planning, Determine the right integration method,

- Train users on how to use the ServiceNow Integration effectively and Ensure Scalability of Integration Solutions

36. ServiceNow Optimization Best Practices

- Activate Process Optimization Plugin and Integrate applications

- Optimize workflows, Process insights & analysis, Create and track optimization tasks

- User Centric Design and prefer Modular Configuration over Heavy Customization

- Accelerate adoption, Reduce total cost of ownership, Increase Productivity, Standardize Processes before Automation

- Effective Knowledge Management and Performance Tuning

- Multi-dimensional processes, Use Best Practice Templates

- Configuration reviews and Integrated continual optimization

37. ServiceNow Compliance and Security Best Practices

- Make sure the security contact details are accurate and always kept up to date

- Ensure that the High Security plugin is installed and activated where possible and enable the "default deny" property

- Consult the ServiceNow Security Center frequently to assess and monitor their instance's overall security level

- Monitor important logs to help identify any suspicious or malicious activity.

- Protect service credentials in a secure storage system

- Encrypt data at rest within the instance using the method that best suits the customer's needs.

- Avoid storing record data on the mobile device

38. ServiceNow Implementation Best Practices

- Define a Roadmap to address Stakeholders and compatibility concerns

- Connect your overall ServiceNow strategy and vision to your implementation plan

- Clearly define short and long-term objectives, Select the right solution, and Use built-in configurations maximum

- Involve stakeholders, Customize Thoughtfully wherever necessary, Monitor and adjust as needed, Go live gradually

- Establish Key Performance Indicators (KPIs), Stating and measuring business goals,

- Map the right process, technology and data to guard against future risk

- Define metrics to track and report against performance, Capture high-visibility

39. Upgrades Management Best Practices

- Planning for Upgrading ServiceNow Strategy, Read the release notes, Evaluate New Features and Functionality,

- Effectively communicate the change across the organization, Schedule Upgrades with the HI Team

- Assess Your Current Environment, Review Customizations

- Plan to Upgrade Production When Usage Is Low

- Check the Upgrade Monitor and Post Upgrade Measures

- Make a backup, Clone Your Sub Production Instances before Upgrading Them, Review Skipped Items

- Streamline future upgrades

40. ServiceNow Issues Management Best Practices

- Identify the issue

- Analyze or vet the issue

- Prioritize the issue

- Determine treatment or resolution

- Execute the steps for resolution

- Track remediation or resolution activities

- Document resolution of the issue

41. ServiceNow Conflict Management Best Practices

- Encourage Open Communication, Talk directly

- Define Clear Roles and Responsibilities

- Set Expectations Early

- Facilitate Regular Team Meetings

- Provide a Constructive Feedback Mechanism

- Create a Positive Team Culture

- Don't blame or name-call, Plan ahead

42. ServiceNow Work Flow Design Best Practices

- Create Flows and Actions in a scoped application

- Avoid Scripted Inputs at All Costs

- Categorize Everything (Flows, Subflows and Actions)

- Use Decision Tables

- Combine Actions in Subflows

- Minimize Subflows Inputs

- NEVER delete a workflow version

43. ServiceNow Team Work Best Practices

- Teamwork makes the DreamWorks

- Adopt a Growth Mindset

- Build an internal team of ServiceNow experts

- ServiceNow + Teamwork Integrations

- Cultivate trust and accountability

- Commitment, Communication and Cooperation

- Clarity, contribution, and concerns

44. ServiceNow Reports Best Practices

- Determine Goals, Objectives, Leading / Lagging Indicators

- Choose clear and concise names for your reports

- Filter and segment data to avoid overloading reports

- Use out-of-the-box reports & ServiceNow Content Packs

- Schedule and automate reports

- Choose best method for sharing reports

- Regularly monitor, review and optimize reports

45. ServiceNow Dashboards Design

- Meet Stakeholders, Gather Dashboards Requirements

- Start with the Outcome in Mind, Build a plan to evolve

- Create personalized and responsive dashboards

- Use Out of the Box Performance Analytics features

- Utilize Visualizations

- Optimize your dashboard's usability

- Share dashboard with user groups rather than individuals

46. Scope Management Best Practices

- Engage Stakeholders, Define Clear Objectives and Scope

- Decide on Desired Outcomes, Customize Thoughtfully

- Contain costs and streamline your project

- Maximizing the return from your investment in ServiceNow

- Use various techniques to manage scope across the project

- Resolve disagreements on scope and project priorities

- Must be aware of potential risks of not managing scope

47. Time Management Best Practices

- Lay Out Your Enterprise Roadmap and Timelines

- Identify, prioritize, and track tasks to be completed

- Activate Time Card Management

- Enable Time Sheet Portal

- Use Time Card Management plugin

- Create a time sheet policy

- Use a time tracker, Record time worked

48. Communication Management Best Practices

- Document communication plan, Set goals early

- Consider messages for all audience levels

- Use multiple communications channels

- Configure Auto Triggers, Notifications and Emails

- Enable Unified Communication as a Service (UCaaS)

- Communicate transparently, frequently and be specific

- Communications doesn't stop after rollout

49. Data Quality Management Best Practices

- Outline Underlying Data Needed for Optimal Success

- Define Metrics of Success and Optimize business processes

- Import data on each instance separately

- Clean data before migration to use right data

- Automate data entry and perform routine data audits

- Enable data culture, consider metadata for data sets

- Data quality trust in Security, Relevancy, and Precision

50. Stakeholders Management Best Practices

- Identify Stakeholders to develop a stakeholder list

- Purposeful stakeholder analysis, assessment and mapping

- Communicate effectively to identify their expectations

- Plan Stakeholder Engagement in decision making

- Reduce Gap between Project Status and Stakeholders

- Communicate Project Challenges to Stakeholders

- and Develop strong stakeholder relations

51. Risk Management Best Practices

- Organize categories of risks across project

- Risk Workspace, consistently assess risks

- Report on financial / statistical impact of risks

- Explore Data Relationships to Reduce Business Risk

- Continuously detect, mitigate, and monitor Risks

- Enable GRC maturity through Risk Portal

- Increases operational stability to decreases legal liability

52. ServiceNow Agile Best Practices

- Enable ServiceNow plugin named "Agile Development 2.0"

- Create sprint backlog and release plan in planning meeting

- Encouraging self-organizing teams to create stability and innovations

- Maintain charts to monitor progress

- Sprint retrospectives to learn from the previous sprint

- Sprint reviews to present work, Eliminate Waste

- Cooperation with a client using Iterative improvements

53. ServiceNow Scrum Best Practices

- Set the main goal for each sprint, ensure Stakeholders participation

- Use Scrum board, Walk the Board

- Create Backlog and Estimates while keeping Stakeholders in loop

- Nurture remote communication, Practice stand-ups, literally

- Plan a new sprint only when the backlog has enough items

- Do not stretch or cut short sprint timings

- Set time aside daily for risk mitigation, Tracking and predicting

54. Test-Driven Development

- Focus on one feature or one aspect at a time

- Make sure each test fails initially

- Write a test before writing production code

- Have a good decent naming convention

- Write independent tests and Write short tests

- Tests should run quickly

- To reduce coupling, use test doubles

55. ServiceNow Daily Standups Meetings Best Practices

- Make sure all team members participate including remote

- Clearly define the purpose or agenda and Keep it short and focused

- Establish a clear leader, appreciate your team's accomplishments

- Use a checklist for more effective stand-up meetings

- Identify roadblocks

- Set aside time for feedback after

- Use templates to inspire and guide your next stand-up

56. ServiceNow Dev Ops Best Practices

- Implement CI/CD, continuous integration/continuous deployment

- Build a culture of collaboration

- Never give up quality for increased speed

- Automate wherever possible, Monitor continuously

- Prioritize observability

- Focus on concepts first, and then find the right tools

- Keep up with documentation and information sharing

57. ServiceNow Data Migration Best Practices

- Design Data migration Scope, Strategy, Migration Realistic time frame

- Build your solution, Brief your key stakeholders

- Make data "fit for purpose", Selecting the Right Tools and Vendors

- Analyze and clean your source data, Create backup of the Data

- Reduce Data loss, Downtime, and business disruption

- Post data migration, ensure that data is complete, translated correctly

- Keep synchronizing data across systems, databases, apps, & devices

58. ServiceNow Service Catalog Design Best Practices

- Take a strategic approach, create the top-level catalog structure

- Identify, organize, and define Items properties

- Define service catalog security, Use Server Side for Data Validation

- Utilize of Item Designer, Simplify and standardize fulfillment workflows

- Make service catalog functional for users, define its maintenance process

- Reduce Efforts with Variable Sets, Don't leave items untagged

- Integrate your service catalog with your self-service portal

59. ServiceNow Service Portal Development Best Practices

- Make your portal appealing to the customers

- Easy Navigation, Make your Service portal device friendly

- Provide enough information

- Embed a widget rather than clone when possible

- Avoid using tags in HTML templates

- Add limits to GlideRecord queries to improve performance

- Use of Route Maps

60. ServiceNow Knowledge Portal Development Best Practices

- Establish guidelines and objectives for content creation and maintenance

- Implement Design Thinking, Content Contextualization, Intelligent Search

- Little Things Matter, Remember that less is more, Consistency is paramount

- Create a community, Make knowledge optimized, digestible, and diverse

- Consolidate Knowledge based on Customer & Agent guided Experience

- Base Your Articles on the Symptoms, Never Make Assumptions

- Provide training and adoption support for continuous improvement

61. HRSD Employment Service Center Best Practices

- Bookmark resources and have a clear vision of what you want to accomplish

- Chart a path to deploy Employment Service Center smooth and easy

- Help your employees to stay engaged, productive, and informed

- Deliver workflows that connect people, functions, and systems

- Provide a single unified Employee Center for employees

- Ensure Lifecycle Journey (on-boarding, off-boarding, and transitions)

- Ensure digital fulfillment of employee inquiries and requests

62. ServiceNow Platform Management/Governance Best Practices

- Build a plan to establish Platform Governance Framework Early

- Invest in Experts for better measurements of performance and successes

- Exploring Instance Scan's capabilities, Plan Regular Instance Health Checks

- Understand what ServiceNow Offers Across the Enterprise

- Stick to the Out-of-the-Box (ITIL) processes

- Highlight best practice violations and recommend solutions

- Continuously Improve Services and Processes

63. ServiceNow Application Development Best Practices

- Define application development strategy and governance requirements

- Choose the Right Methodology and Sticking to a Framework

- Build effective application development processes

- Build application models to respond today and future business needs

- Keeping the Code Simple, Document Code properly, Getting Code Reviews

- Do Thorough Unit Tests and Take Advantage of Issue Tracker

- Manage with Version Control

64. ServiceNow CMDB Best Practices

- Enable CMDB Health dashboard

- Prefer to use OOB CI classes, Use relationship mapping to understand dependencies

- Avoid customization & Use a consistent data model

- CMDB Attribute should be placed at the right level.

- Establish and maintain CMDB governance, regularly review and clean up the CMDB

- Ensure accurate configuration of your IT Discovery process

- Automate data collection and update processes

65. ServiceNow Mid Server Best Practices

- Have a single MID Server tasked with a single purpose e.g. Discovery, Service Mapping, etc.

- Linux or Windows, For Production environments, install one MID Server application per host.

- Deploy the MID Server on a local drive on the host within a unique folder name with no space

- MID Servers required depends on number of targets to interact with and frequency of interaction

- Multiple MID Servers should be separately hosted within each network segment

- Increase the number of threads in the MID Server if you need more patterns and probes.

- Monitor by using the MID Server Dashboard by navigating to MID Server > Dashboard

66. ServiceNow Discovery Best Practices

- Plan the Discovery process, scope, frequency of Discovery, probes and sensors to be used

- Determine the IP range, devices, and applications to be discovered

- Ensure all the credentials required for different devices and applications

- Decide on the frequency of discovery, the time window for discovery, and the order of discovery

- Install the MID Server, configure it to communicate with the ServiceNow instance

- Validate the information in the CMDB is accurate and up-to-date

- Documentation is essential for maintaining compliance and IT environment

67. ServiceNow Integration Hub Best Practices

- Provides a no/low-code approach to integration, making it easier to set up and maintain

- Pre-built spokes for common integrations, reducing the need for custom development.

- Allows for the creation of integration flows using a visual interface, making it more user-friendly

- Built-in error-handling mechanisms for managing and resolving integration issues

- Designed to handle a large number of integrations efficiently.

- Create only one Scoped Application for a Spoke

- Prevent looping when integrating

68. DevOps role in Optimizing Business Agility

- Better alignment of development and operations

- Continuous Integration and Continuous Deployment (CI/CD)

- Validation of configuration management changes

- Improved collaboration, communication, Stability, Security, Speed, Collaboration

- Automation of manual tasks

- Incorporate security at every level with DevSecOps

- Decrease code writing time with DevOps

69. ServiceNow SecOps Best Practices

- The security contacts in the Now Support Portal should always be up to date

- Activate the ServiceNow High Security Plugin and Update Software and Patches

- Frequently monitor instance's security level by consulting ServiceNow's Instance Security Center

- Secure Email Communications, Monitor Sensitive Logs, Avoid potential pitfalls

- Follow Encryption Protocols, Web browsers should be configured to use TLS 1.2 or higher

- For authentication, always use MFA and refrain from storing record data locally on a device

- Enforce MID Server Security, Follow Encryption Protocols

70. ServiceNow SecOps Benefits

- Return on investment

- Security and operations become streamlined

- Reduced resources

- Fewer cloud security issues

- Fewer app disruptions

- Better auditing procedures

71. ServiceNow REST API Best Practices

- Avoid basic authentication and go for OAuth wherever possible

- Set up OAuth profile, make sure you enforce it

- After authenticated, do authorization with the help of ACLs

- Use the appropriate conventions for specific usage

- Use versioning to control changes to your API

- Return Informative HTTP status code and Return useful error information

- Enforce and test access controls, create a good API documentation

72. SOAP API (Simple Object Access Protocol) XML-based protocol

- Use a URL query to request a table's WSDL

- Use import tables and transform maps to automate web service requests for tables

- Use custom JavaScript to execute SOAP web services requests.

- SOAP messages are sent with the assumption that the recipient is XML compliant

- Now Platform supports long-running SOAP requests

- Improves efficiency of ODBC driver when requesting large numbers of records

- To use SOAP web services, you must have the appropriate role for the operation

73. ServiceNow Data Migration Best Practices

- Proper planning and scoping are crucial for a successful migration.

- Prepare your instance for migration before you start the migration activity

- Identify and evaluate current legacy system & determine scope of migration

- Before migration, clean/optimize data to eliminate duplicates & inconsistencies

- Perform rigorous testing of migration process in non-production environment

- Monitor performance and optimization in the migration process in real-time

- Always have a backup plan in case of unforeseen issues or data corruption

74. ServiceNow Orchestration Best Practices

- Creating a security automation and orchestration strategy

- The More MID Servers, the Better

- For Implementation, Give Yourself More Time than You Think You Need

- Leverage Multiple 'Discovery' Tools to Complete Your CMDB

- Know Which Alerts You Want

- Orchestration: If You Can Dream It, You Can Do It

- IT Operations Management Can Be Much More Out-of-the-Box

75. ServiceNow Scripting Best Practices

- Write efficient scripts that minimize database queries

- Utilize Script Includes for reusable functions

- Employ client-side scripting for a better user experience

- Implement proper error handling in scripts

- Avoid hardcoding sensitive information like passwords or API keys in scripts

76. Client Script Best Practices

- Well-designed Client Scripts can improve the user experience.

- Avoid global Client Scripts, Run only necessary client scripts

- Avoid using DOM (manipulating elements via the Document Object Model)

- Never use GlideRecord in Client Scripts

- Wrap code in functions, restrict list editing, Minimize server lookups

- Avoid using GlideRecord queries in client side scripts

- Avoid using synchronous AJAX methods in client side scripts

77. Server Script Best Practices

- Avoid Null or Undefined variables in GlideRecord

- Manage large arrays or objects as they can cause many specific failure

- De-referencing unneeded variables

- Avoid spawning too much work, too quickly

- Use asynchronous methods on server when a transaction is waiting for response

- Limit the number of returned records when querying very large tables.

- Avoid running out of memory due to storing dot-walked GlideElement fields

78. UI Policies Best Practices

- UI policies dynamically change behavior of information on a form

- Basic UI policies do not require scripting, use Run scripts option for advanced actions

- The order of UI Policies does matter. The lower the order, the higher the priority.

- Make sure your UI Policy conditions are not conflicting with each other.

- If your form is very complex, consider using client scripts instead of UI Policies.

- Document your form behavior and the logic behind it

- Always test your form behavior thoroughly

79. UI Actions Best Practices

- UI actions simplify processes and guide user activity on forms and lists.

- Create well-designed UI actions

- Give each UI action a distinct action name

- Use conditions in UI actions

- Use buttons, menus, and links appropriately in forms and lists.

- Leverage business rules

- Leverage script includes

80. Business Rules Best Practices

- Keep business rules simple and focused

- Avoid using business rules for complex logic

- Use the before and after business rule types appropriately

- Use conditions to narrow the scope of your business rules

- Prevent Recursive Business Rules, Using script includes instead of global business rules

- Keep Code in functions, avoiding client-callable business rules.

- Use logging to troubleshoot issues, Test your business rules thoroughly

81. Data Policies Best Practices

- Data policies enable to enforce data consistency by setting mandatory & read-only fields

- A Data Policy execute on the server side but can also run as a UI Policy on the client side

- Data Policies are applied to all data entered into the platform

- Purpose of a Data Policy is to standardize the same data across ServiceNow applications

- Data Policies have a unique purpose in ServiceNow, just like UI Policies and ACLs

- Convert a data policy to a UI policy if a data policy already exists

- You can create a new data policy to define data rules for a table

82. Data Dictionary Best Practices

- A Data Dictionary is a description/data model of a piece of information (Object).

- Includes key components such as term names, definitions, data types, & allowable values

- Begin by establishing a clear and consistent structure for your data dictionary

- Contain information about the data source and related terms

- Also contains any calculations or transformations the data may undergo.

- Use Dictionary Overrides to change field settings on extended tables

- The frequency of updates to a data dictionary should align with Org's data environment

83. Data Model and Database Best Practices

- Design a clean and efficient data model using appropriate tables, fields, and relationships.

- Normalize the database where appropriate to avoid data redundancy.

- Avoid creating too many custom tables unless necessary.

84. Release Management Best Practices

- Define and document your Release Management process, Clearly define success criteria

- Tailor the release management process to meet Client needs

- Consider a dark launch, testing it in a real-world setting before a public release

- Automate processes

- Track metrics

- Review launches, Reduce user impact

- Imitate production environments

85. Incident Management Best Practices

- Define Clear Incident Management Policies and Procedures:

- Automate Routine Tasks and Workflows

- Implement Robust Monitoring and Alerting Mechanisms

- Promote Cross-Functional Collaboration and Knowledge Sharing

- Monitor Performance Metrics and KPIs

- Resolution notes should include all steps leading to the resolution

- Conduct a post-incident analysis to identify the root causes

86. Problem Management Best Practices

- Identify gaps in your current process and supporting tools

- Collaborate with stakeholders to understand process requirements

- Define and document your Problem Management process

- Capture user stories and requirements to guide the developer

- Ensure sustainability by providing ITSM training

- Define controls, reporting metrics, and implementing governance

- Maintaining a proactive Problem Management process is essential

87. Problem Management Life Cycle

- Problem Detection

- Categorize and Prioritize

- Investigate and Diagnose

- Resolve and close the problem

- Major problem review

88. Change Management Best Practices

- Create Change Management Service Strategy and change calendar

- Establish a robust change approval process

- Align people and processes

- Ensure User Adoption

- Involve as many stakeholders as is possible or reasonable

- Regularly communicate change updates & progress to stakeholders

- Continuously evaluate & improve change management process

89. Change Management Life Cycle

- Create Change Request

- Review Change

- Change Evaluation

- Change Approvals

- Implementation

- Validation

90. Case Management (HRSD) Life Cycle

- Initiation

- Intake and Categorization

- Assignment and Prioritization

- Investigation and Collaboration

- Resolution

- Closure

- Feedback and Continuous Improvement

91. Virtual Agent Best Practices

- Identify Your Goals

- Tackle the Most Common Issues First

- Personalize the Greetings

- Be Down to the Point, keep the topics narrow and clear

- Incorporate a Fallback Topic

- Address Data Protection Issues

- Measure the Results

92. Robotic Process Automation (RPA) Best Practices

- Begin with a high-level framework

- Break down processes into specific workflows

- Choose activities carefully

- Increase workflow readability

- Store reusable components

- Build in error handling

- Create configurable files

93. Continual Service Improvement Management Best Practices

- Start small, show value achieved and build improvement culture

- Distribute responsibility for CSI throughout the organization

- Proactively identify improvement opportunities

- Log and track improvement opportunities in CSI registers

- Align your improvement with strategy

- Measure impact & share improvement achieved with the team

- Go beyond just Improving Services or Processes

94. Reporting vs Analytics

- Reporting shows current state

- Data as discrete facts

- Reporting doesn't predict future

- Analytics shows trends

- Relationships between data sets

- Analytics predict future outcomes

95. Performance Optimization Best Practices

- Monitor system performance and address performance issues promptly.

- Monitor and optimize instance performance to enhance user experience.

- Use indexing and database optimization techniques.

- Avoid running expensive server scripts excessively.

- Use performance monitoring tools available in ServiceNow.

96. ServiceNow Managed Services for Customers

- Application development for enhancements

- Backlog reduction and overflow support

- Production support and system administration

- Architecture and platform optimization

- Version upgrades

- Manual and automated testing

98. Essential Resources for ServiceNow Professionals

- ServiceNow Community

- Developer Program

- Product Documentation

- Now Learning

- Now Create

- Personal Developer Instance

- SNDevs Slack

- ServiceNow Developers Discord

- ServiceNow YouTube Channels

97. ServiceNow Best Practices to Drive Customer Experience

- Establish a Solid Service Strategy

- Align People, Processes and Technology

- Build ServiceNow Foundation

- Drive User Adoption

- Revisit Your Strategy Regularly

SCCM	(System Center Configuration Manager)
SDLC	(Software Development Life Cycle)
SecOps	(Security Operations)
SIR	(Security Incident Response)
SLA	(Service Level Agreement)
SM	(Service Mapping)
SNPI	(ServiceNow Platform Implementation)
SOAP	(Simple object access protocol)
SP	(Service Provider)
SQL	(Structured Query Language)
SSO	(Single Sign-On)
UAT	(User Acceptance Testing)
UI	(User Interface)
URIs	(Uniform Resource Identifiers)
URL	(Uniform Resource Locators)
UX	(User Experience)
VA	(Virtual Agents)
VMs	(Virtual Machines)
VR	(Vulnerability Response)
VRM	(Vendor Risk Management)
W3C	(World Wide Web Consortium)
WebDAV	(Web Distributed Authoring and Versioning)
WSDL	(Web Service Description Language)
XML	(Extensible Markup Language)
XSLT	(Extensible Stylesheet Language Transformations)

HTML	(Hyper Text Markup Language)
IaaS	(Infrastructure-as-a-Service)
IRE	(Identification and Reconciliation Engine)
ITAM	(IT Assets Management)
ITBM	(IT Business Management)
ITIL	(IT Infrastructure Library)
ITOM	(IT Operations Management)
ITSM	(IT Services Management)
JDBC	(Java Database Connectivity)
JSON	(JavaScript Object Notation)
KB	(Knowledge Base)
KCS	(Knowledge-Centered Service)
KPIs	(Key Performance Indicators)
LDAP	(Lightweight Directory Access Protocol)
MAM	(Mobile Application Management)
MDM	(Mobile Device Management)
OLA	(Operations Level Agreement)
OOAD	(Object Oriented Analysis and Design)
OOB	(Out of the Box)
PaaS	(Platforms-as-a-Service)
PL/SQL	(Procedural Language for SQL)
PPM	(Project Portfolio Management)
PPM	(Project Portfolio Management)
RC	(Risk & Compliance)
REST	(RESTful)
SaaS	(Software-as-a-Service)
SAM	(Software Asset Management)
SAML	(Security Assertion Markup Language)

AJAX	(Asynchronous JavaScript And XML)
API	(Application Program Interface)
APM	(Application Portfolio Management)
AWS	(Amazon Web Service)
CAD	(Certified Application Developer)
CAS	(Certified Application Specialist)
CAS-PA	(Certified Application Specialist – Performance Analytics)
CCS	(Catalog Client Scripts)
CEs	(Underpinning Contracts)
CIs	(Configuration Items)
CIS	(Certified Implementation Specialist)
CMDB	(Configuration Management Database)
COE	(Center of Excellence)
CPG	(Cloud Provisioning and Governance)
CR	(Change Request)
CRUD	(Create, Read, Update, Delete)
CSA	(Certified System Administrator)
CSM	(Customer Services Management)
CSS	(Custom Style Sheets)
Disco	(Discovery)
EM	(Event Management)
FMA	(Multi-Factor Authentication)
FSM	(Field Service Management)
FTPS	(Secure File Transfer Protocol)
GRC	(Governance Risk and Compliance)
HAM	(Hardware Asset Management)
HRSD	(HR Service Delivery)

Glossary

100. Documentation

- Maintain thorough documentation for configurations, customizations, and scripts.

- This documentation should include comments in scripts, descriptions in fields, and detailed records of configurations.

99. User Training

- Provide training to users and administrators to ensure they understand how to use the platform effectively.

- This can reduce errors and improve efficiency.

www.ingramcontent.com/pod-product-compliance
Lightning Source LLC
LaVergne TN
LVHW051702050326
832903LV00032B/3965